Original title:
Rose-Scented Rhetoric

Copyright © 2025 Creative Arts Management OÜ
All rights reserved.

Author: Dorian Ashford
ISBN HARDBACK: 978-1-80567-057-5
ISBN PAPERBACK: 978-1-80567-137-4

The Language of Lilies

In the garden where blooms chatter,
Lilies gossip like they matter.
'Oh, did you hear what Daisy said?'
'No, but I saw what she fed!'

Petals flutter, secrets shared,
While bees hum tunes, completely unprepared.
A tulip trips, a daffodil laughs,
And roses roll their petals, taking their halves.

Charming blooms in fierce debate,
'Who wore the best color? Which is first-rate?'
While violets quietly plot and scheme,
Their world's a stage, or so it would seem.

In this floral circus of banter bright,
Each fragrant character knows their plight.
With leafy fists, they throw their shade,
Making laughter bloom where whispers invade.

Floral Footprints

In a meadow where daisies dance,
Bees create a buzzing romance.
'You won't believe what I saw last night,'
Said the pansy, trying to take flight.

Tulips tease the shy sunflowers,
'Let's have blooms, not boring hours!'
While snapdragons grin with glee,
Playing tricks like it's meant to be.

Every petal is a clever joke,
Each odor a quip, a fragrant poke.
Lavender winks, 'I'm the calm one,'
But even I can't skip the fun run.

So come, let's wander this floral path,
Where laughter's found in nature's wrath.
In every footprint, a story's told,
In this blooming farce, watch smiles unfold.

Sweetened Rhetoric

Whispers that tickle the ears,
With laughter, they dance through the years.
Sweet words like candy, oh what a treat,
Making life's troubles feel light on our feet.

Jokes wrapped in petals, so charming and bright,
They brighten the day, a delightful sight.
A sprinkle of humor in every bouquet,
Turning mundane talks into a playful ballet.

Floral Phantoms in Dialogue

Invisible blooms with a witty flair,
Spouting nonsense like they just don't care.
Chasing each other in jest and delight,
Their giggles can echo into the night.

Petals of laughter, they float in the air,
Bantering blooms have no need for despair.
With each quip, they blossom and sway,
In a garden of humor, forever they play.

Notes of Nectar

Each word drips sweetness, a sugary sound,
Like bees buzzing softly, they swirl all around.
Sipping on laughter, they nectarize prose,
Drenched in amusement, it overflows.

Melodies flutter like bees in bloom,
Witty remarks chase away all the gloom.
In the hive of delight, the fun never stops,
With every great jest, the chuckles just pop.

Petal-Laden Proclamations

Proclaiming with petals, a comical flair,
They shout from the rooftops, with joy to share.
Jubilant giggles erupt like a rose,
In the garden of laughter, everyone knows.

With proclamations so silly, they laugh and they dance,
Transforming mere moments into a chance.
Petals of humor twirling in glee,
In the circus of chatter, they flourish, you see!

Botanicals and Banter

In the garden of chatter, petals collide,
With giggles and snickers, blooming with pride.
A daisy drops puns, while tulips just tease,
Violets roll laughter, like bumblebees sneeze.

The sun blushes brightly, leaves start to sway,
As jokes take root, growing wild every day.
Sprouts of humor dance 'neath the seasonal light,
With blooms gossiping sweetly, oh what a sight!

Blooms of Belief

Trust the lilacs, they know all the facts,
While daisies debate what color attracts.
Sunflowers nod wisely, with serious grace,
Yet poppies just giggle, 'What's truth in this space?'

In laughter they blossom, belief takes the floor,
With hilarity woven, who could ask for more?
A patch of absurdity, all in good fun,
Where petals and puns bask in the sun!

The Scent of Solace

In the corner of laughter, whiffs of delight,
A floral concoction that tickles the night.
Forget all your troubles, just follow the scent,\nWith jasmine concoctions and humor well-spent.

A whiff of absurd, as the daisies conspire,
While lavender comforts, like jokes on a wire.
In gardens of giggles, solace is found,
Where blooms whisper secrets that dance all around.

Colours of Cognition

Mind blooming bright like marigold's hue,
With thoughts intertwining, all fresh and anew.
Petals of wisdom, in shades of delight,
Highlighting the follies that spark in the night.

A spectrum of humor, each color a pun,
As laughter erupts and shines like the sun.
In a patch of insight, where joy doesn't cease,
The brain plays with colors, and finds its own peace.

Scented Verses on a Summer Breeze

On a warm day, words take flight,
Tickling noses, laughter in sight.
Jokes blossom like flowers in bloom,
Whispers dance, chasing away gloom.

A bumblebee buzzes with flair,
Its jokes land softly, light as air.
With every giggle, petals spread,
Silly tales filling hearts, they're wed.

Nectar of Nuance

Sipping sweetness from clever puns,
Each twist and turn, oh, how it runs!
Quotes drip like honey on toast,
Highlighting humor we treasure most.

Punning bees share their golden stash,
Words whirl around like a friendly flash.
With every chuckle, joy's unveiled,
Innuendos dance, never derailed.

Vines of Rhetoric Entwined

In tangled vines where laughter grows,
Wit winds round, and anything goes.
Debate me here, I'll tease and jest,
Flowery phrases are simply the best!

Playful jabs like petals they throw,
Bursting forth in a vibrant show.
With each exchange, their truth is found,
Riddles petal-soft, laughter abound.

Aromatic Arguments Under the Moon

Under the stars, we bicker and play,
Amusing thoughts drift on display.
Each assertion a fragrant delight,
Chasing shadows in the soft moonlight.

With quirky quips and cheeky retorts,
Amid the night, we craft our courts.
Each phrase a burst of playful glee,
In this debate, let's sip on tea!

Violets Whispering Hidden Depths

Violets giggle with delight,
Their secrets float in the night.
Beneath each tale, they slyly weave,
Jokes hidden well, for us to believe.

Petals brush against my cheek,
Whispers soft, but oh so cheek!
They laugh at woes of old and gray,
In violet hues, they jest and play.

The Scent of Sophistry

A whiff of stories, bold and bright,
Crafted tales take sudden flight.
With every whiff, the truth can bend,
Like a twisty vine that won't quite end.

Perfumed words hug the air so well,
Desire to buy what they compel.
Puns and wit in every spray,
Sophistry dancing about all day.

Perfume of Persuasion

Spray the charm and cast the net,
A scent that no one can forget.
With each dab of this sly perfume,
Arguments blossom, drawing doom!

A whiff that whispers, 'Come on, try!'
While subtly hinting, 'Don't ask why.'
Floral antics on the breeze,
Persuasion swirls with such great ease.

Pollen and Prose: A Harmonious Blend

Pollen drifts on afternoon air,
Tickling noses everywhere.
Prose flutters in colorful dreams,
Both are more than they might seem.

Buzzing bees take to the stage,
In playful dance, they turn the page.
With laughter sweet as flower's cheer,
Words and pollen bring us near.

Aromatic Artistry

A painter with noses for flair,
Mixes aromas with utmost care.
The canvas smells sweet, oh what a trick,
As he swirls his brush, the bubbles stick.

Colors of cinnamon and mint collide,
What a masterpiece, some say, 'why hide?'
The critics can't breathe, they've laughed too hard,
His fragrant delight, a whiffing bard.

The Scented Canvas

In a gallery where smells take flight,
The paintings giggle, oh what a sight!
Each brushstroke bursts with a whiff of fun,
A glimmer of lemon, and look—the sun!

Artists debate, 'Is that grape or peach?'
While the audience munches on sweets to teach.
With laughter and scents, the room's aglow,
Who knew art could have such a show?

Symphony of the Subtle Fragrance

A symphony plays in a fragrant hall,
Notes of vanilla dance, rise, and fall.
A clarinet sneezes, it's a funny affair,
As the audience giggles at the sweetened air.

Each instrument wafts a peculiar scent,
Making the conductor slightly bent.
With laughter in tune, they sing and rhyme,
Who knew fragrances could so delight time?

Blooming Rhetoric

In a garden where words bloom and strut,
Petals whisper secrets, each word a nut.
A tulip teases with a roguish wink,
While daisies chuckle, oh how they stink!

Conversations are fragrant, ripe with glee,
As bees buzz along with a whimsical spree.
The leaves roll their eyes at the poets' lines,
In this flowery debate, the humor shines.

Charms in the Breeze

A breeze sauntered by, with a wink and a grin,
It whispered sweet things, like a cheeky young kin.
"You smell like a garden!" it giggled with glee,
"And news of your charms, oh, they travel with me!"

Butterflies hovered, as if caught in a dance,
In petals they twirled, with each fleeting chance.
"Don't take it to heart, just a flirt of the air,
For gravel's got blooms that can hardly compare!"

Flora and Phrase

In the land of the chatty, where flowers confide,
Petunias gossip while daisies provide.
"Did you hear the news?" chirped a daisy so bright,
"I bloomed in a garden, and sprouted some height!"

A tulip chimed in, with a flourish of flair,
"But I'm more fragrant! You can't help but stare!"
They traded sweet quips with each soft, tender sigh,
As bees took their chances, all buzzing nearby.

Whispers in the Wind

The wind sings a tune, a little off-key,
It pokes fun at the trees, and all braves with glee.
"Your leaves look a tad shabby, dear spruces, don't pout!"

"Just wait till I make my grand exit, no doubt!"

Tulips burst out with a colorful cheer,
"We bloom in the sunlight; that's our time of year!"
But the wind only chuckled, as it flitted on by,
"Oh flowers, you're cute, but I'm the real high-fly!"

Language in Bloom

In a field full of chatter, each bloom has a word,
They laugh at the silence, for it's simply absurd.
"I can rhyme with a breeze!" said a daffodil spry,
"And dance at the stars till the moon says goodbye!"

A violet chuckled, with petals aflame,
"You can't beat my vibrance, we're all just the same!"
"Yet each of us whispers a tale from the ground,
In our flowered assembly, strange humor is found!"

Whispers in Bloom

In the garden, laughter sings,
Petals chuckle on soft wings.
Bees are conspiring in sweet chatter,
While blooms debate on what does matter.

Sunny jokes make flowers sway,
Tulips sip tea in a comical way.
Daisies giggle, sharing a pun,
Nature's humor can't be outrun.

Butterflies tease the bumblebees,
Tickling them with a gentle breeze.
The daisies dance, their petals flare,
Whispers of joy fill the air.

In vibrant hues, the jokes unfold,
Stories of petals daring and bold.
Each bloom a jest, a punchline bright,
In this laughter, the world feels light.

Scented Soliloquies

Lilies chat with a fragrant grace,
A rose winks, oh what a face!
With scents like gossip, they enthrall,
Conversations rise, and petals call.

Jasmine giggles, sweet perfume,
While violets plot a grand costume.
Their drama blooms with every tease,
In flowery gowns that dance in the breeze.

Pansies whisper of the best blooms,
While marigolds mourn in dusty rooms.
Every scent carries tales to share,
In this fragrant play, joy fills the air.

Amidst the fragrance, secrets combine,
Chasing clouds with jokes divine.
A floral stage set just for fun,
Where laughter grows under the sun.

Declarations in Lavender

Lavender speaks with a soothing tone,
Its gentle laughter, sweetly grown.
In fields of purple, cheeky puns,
Playful verses under golden suns.

A dainty sigh, a fragrant jest,
Rosemary chiming in with zest.
Sprigs of thyme join in the fight,
Making spice of each delight.

With each bouquet a jest is told,
Citrusy hints that never grow old.
These declarations bring delight,
In lavender fields, everything feels right.

In the air, a comical flair,
Flora giggles, scent everywhere.
From bloom to bloom, the humor flows,
In this aromatic world, joy only grows.

The Aroma of Eloquence

Whiffs of wit, a fragrant delight,
Each sentient flower, eloquent in flight.
Petals paint pictures, colors abound,
With every sniff, sweet humor is found.

Charming daisies recite in rhyme,
While peonies boast of fragrant thyme.
The aroma swirls in comedic grace,
As flora dances in this floral space.

Cheerful blossoms share their tales,
Of silly bees and wind that wails.
In this garden, laughter spills,
With jokes that tickle like summer thrills.

The scent of humor fills the air,
In a world where joy is everywhere.
Each bloom a quip, a fragrant cheer,
Inviting all to come near.

The Linguistic Lilt of Lilacs

Words dance like petals in the breeze,
Whispers of laughter amid buzzing bees.
Puns float down from the lilac's crown,
Tickling the ears of the quick and the brown.

In a garden of phrases, bright and absurd,
Each phrase a flower, each laugh a bird.
Chasing away frowns with each fruity quip,
A bouquet of giggles on a whimsical trip.

Metaphors bloom like vibrant sights,
Luring in giggles, igniting delights.
With a sprinkle of charm and a twist of delight,
Every word's a petal in the warm sunlight.

So come take a stroll through this fragrant field,
Where laughter and language are playfully sealed.
With lilacs and chuckles, it's pure sensory joy,
Join in the fun, oh dear girl and boy!

Aromatic Allusions

In the kitchen of wit, we stir up some fun,
A dash of absurdity until we are done.
Similes simmer while humor is grilled,
One taste of the punchline, our senses are thrilled.

Sprigs of sarcasm garnish the plate,
As laughter bubbles, we're never too late.
With aromatic chaos, we season our talk,
Creating a feast, just follow the squawk.

Peppered with puns and spicy delight,
Conversations sizzle under soft twilight.
In this kitchen of chatter, we whip up a storm,
Where laughter is key, and all minds transform.

So bring out the flavors, let's make it a bash,
Let's blend up our words with a quick little splash.
These allusions are fragrant, a humorous tease,
Come feast on the fun, it'll put you at ease!

Harmony of Herbaceous Hues

In a garden of giggles where laughter's the hue,
Herbs share their secrets, a comedy brew.
Thyme whispers jokes while the basil will cheer,
Chives cut through frowns, it's a dish full of cheer.

With a sprinkle of parsley and a dash of dill,
Every conversation has flavor to fill.
Gather round folks, let the herbs take the lead,
In this fragrant arena, we all plant a seed.

The rosemary chuckles, the mint is so sly,
While sage stands by, letting humor fly high.
Like a salad of banter, let it all blend,
The harmony grows as we laugh without end.

So dance with our produce, let's flourish and sway,
Together we'll frolic, come join in the play.
In the garden of giggles, we all get our due,
With herbaceous humor, our friendships renew!

Petals and Proverbs

Oh, the petals that tumble, like wisdom laid bare,
Proverbs awaken, swirling sweet in the air.
With a knowing wink and a laugh so sincere,
We catch these delights as they drift ever near.

"Don't count the petals on a flower so bright,
Instead count the laughs that can lighten the night."
Every saying a petal, each chuckle a stem,
In this garden of laughter, let's honor them then.

"Wherever you wander, let humor be gold,
For jokes shared in sunshine are never too old."
In the realm of the witty, we bloom every day,
Finding joy in the quips that life throws our way.

So gather the proverbs like blossoms in spring,
As laughter and wisdom join in a ring.
In this charming bouquet, we'll forever reside,
With petals of joy, our humor our guide!

Whispers of Floral Persuasion

In gardens where jesters sing,
Petals prance with foolish fling.
With every giggle, blooms sway,
Logic dances, then runs away.

Cacti shush, they sharpen pricks,
While daisies toss all the quick tricks.
A tulip winks, oh what a tease,
Who knew blooms could breeze with such ease?

Pansies laugh beneath the sun,
As bees chuckle, 'Oh, what fun!'
Each whisper crafted, soft and sweet,
Pleading hearts to skip a beat.

Petals of Poetic Discourse

Let's argue in a garden patch,
Where daisies fling their clever catch.
The sunflowers boast of grand debates,
While violets muse on love's fates.

Charming blooms, they squabble bright,
As butterflies join in the fight.
They prattle on in bloom-filled glee,
Words as fragrant as you can see.

Clever phrases, petals twist,
A daisy-boy can't resist!
Negotiate with floral wit,
In this friendly floral bit.

The Aroma of Forgotten Words

Forgotten phrases waft through air,
Like sunflowers that don't play fair.
A whiff of laughter, the scent of tease,
Makes daisies bounce, gives humor ease.

Fragrant whispers float on breeze,
Lilies chuckle, oh how they please!
They say 'remember', but who can tell?
When humor blooms, all goes so well.

Chortling petals, they can't stay mute,
Sipping nectar, they raise a flute.
With every laugh, a bud peeks out,
Mixing joy with a hint of doubt.

Scented Arguments in Bloom

Arguments sprout in colors bright,
As tulips tussle with all their might.
Petal combat, a playful scene,
With laughter swirling like a dream.

Violets chirp their witty lines,
While daisies quote the sun's designs.
A silly squabble in flower groove,
Watch their petals jive and move.

Laughter echoes in vibrant hues,
As lilacs sing their clever views.
In this bloom-filled banter spree,
All arguments smell sweet, you see!

The Scented Symphony

In a garden where giggles grow,
A symphony of scents, quite the show,
Bees buzz tunes on a fragrant quest,
While ants tap dance, they're looking their best.

The daisies hum, the lilies cheer,
"Sniff us all, don't you dare fear!"
Lilac laughs, "I'm sweet, not shy,"
Falling petals, winking as they fly.

A thistle quips, "I'm sharp, it's true,
But I'll gladly join this merry crew!"
And in this garden, scents collide,
A fragrant circus, let's enjoy the ride!

Even the soil gives a hearty chortle,
As roots share gossip, their little portal,
A whiff of fun in every breeze,
A scented symphony, if you please!

Blooming Ballads

In fields where flowers strut and sway,
They sing their tunes in a bright bouquet,
"Join our chorus, it's flower power!"
The sun beams down, a cheerful flower.

Petunias prance with a charming grin,
"Life's too short, let the fun begin!"
Sunflowers spin like they're at a ball,
While tulips giggle, causing a brawl.

Daffodils chant with a joyful flair,
"Pick me, pick me! Show how you care!"
In this garden of melody and mirth,
Every bloom celebrates its birth.

So come along, dance in the sun,
With blooming ballads, laughter's the fun,
A whistle here, a giggle there,
Joy in every corner, everywhere!

Hue of Human Harmony

In a garden, colors clash and play,
Each petal tells tales in a funny way,
"Look at me!" shouts a bright daffodil,
"Unicorns envy my sunshine thrill!"

Violets murmur, "We're just too cool,
With our royal hues, we rule this school!"
The marigolds boast, "We're spicy and bold,
With laughter in leaves, our stories unfold."

Every hue joins in the comic fight,
"I'm pink, I'm splashy, you'll find me right!"
The blues chime in, "We're calm yet grand,
In this riot of colors, we all stand hand in hand."

A palette of fun, a canvas aglow,
In this blooming chaos, watch the joy flow,
Each shade echoes laughter, a melody sweet,
Celebrating unity, no small feat!

Bright Bouquets of Being

In a vase where the chuckles reside,
A bouquet of fun sits side by side,
"Smile wide!" cries the dahlia delight,
As roses wink in the soft daylight.

"Life can be silly!" the geranium grins,
With petals aglow where humor begins,
"Oh, pick me!" demands a bold snapdragon,
"Life's for laughing, don't be a wag-on!"

The cosmos twirl in a whimsical dance,
"Grab a buddy, take a silly chance!"
With violets giggling under the sun,
In bright bouquets, we're all having fun!

So let's celebrate with laughter and cheer,
In fragrant blossoms, we hold our dear,
A bright bouquet, a giggle parade,
Together we bond, our joy never fades!

The Aroma of Aspiration

In gardens where dreams take flight,
We bloom with ideas, oh what a sight!
With petals of hope, we strut our stuff,
Who knew ambition could smell so tough?

Daisies giggle, they think it's a joke,
While tulips whisper, 'You're all just smoke!'
But violets nod, they're always supportive,
They know success is a floral sportitive!

Climbing the trellis, our hopes intertwine,
Like ivy and blossoms, all acting divine.
With a whiff of laughter, we reach for the stars,
And leave behind the scent of our scars!

So here's to the blooms, may they never wilt,
In the race of aspiration, we're always built.
With every whiff of humor, we thrive,
And chuckle as we dance, feeling so alive!

Floral Metaphors in Motion

Pansies paint pictures with every frown,
While roses in skirts spin round and round.
Petunias prance with a swagger so bold,
But lilies just gossip, oh how they scold!

The daisies debate, which way is the sun?
The squirrels are judges; they're having some fun!
With laughter that drips like nectar so sweet,
These floral metaphors just can't be beat!

Orchids offer wisdom, but only in rhyme,
While daisies declare it's their party time.
The blooms are all laughing, it's quite the fest,
With petals of laughter, they're simply the best!

So let's dance with the flowers, as life rolls along,
In a meadow of metaphors, we'll sing our song.
With laughter in blossoms and joy to unfurl,
Let's throw a bouquet and give Spring a twirl!

Harmony of Blossoms

In a garden where chuckles bloom side by side,
The tulips are tickled, the daisies collide.
With giggles and grins, they dance in the breeze,
Creating a symphony, putting us at ease.

The sunflowers stand tall, with smiles so wide,
As the violets tease, 'Come join the fun ride!'
Buttercups bounce in their polka-dot suits,
While the roses crack jokes and share their roots.

In this floral fiesta, there's no room for gloom,
With rhythms of sunshine, we all start to bloom.
A symphony's playing, each petal's a note,
As laughter weaves gently on a fragrant boat.

So gather the blossoms in a flowery gang,
Let's revel in friendship where laughter will clang.
In harmony blooming, we'll dance through the day,
With petals of humor, we'll laugh all the way!

Springtime Surrealism

In a land where daisies wear top hats and bow ties,
And the bees pull pranks with hilarious flies.
The daffodils giggle at clouds made of cheese,
While rabbits in coats poke fun at the breeze.

Cherries throw parties, where raindrops act shy,
While sunbeams perform acrobatics up high.
The tulips, they sulk, thinking they're misunderstood,
But they can't resist smiling, it's all quite good!

With blossoms in suits, they waltz hand in hand,
Inviting the wind to join in their band.
The peonies blaze in an uproarious tune,
As laughter and petals dance under the moon.

So let's paint the sky with our wildest delight,
And savor each moment, from morning to night.
In this surreal garden where nothing goes wrong,
We'll giggle with flowers and sing our own song!

Serenade of the Scented Speech

In a garden of chatter, blooms of delight,
Words dance like petals, taking flight.
They chatter and giggle, a floral parade,
Sprinkling humor in every charade.

Laughter like pollen, it drifts through the air,
Tickling your senses without a care.
A dimpled retort, a chuckle so sweet,
Twirling like daisies on tiny, swift feet.

Jokes that unfurl like buds in the spring,
Conversations that twinkle, and merrily sing.
Each quip a fragrance, absurdly bizarre,
In this silly symposium where puns are the star.

A blushing bouquet of banter takes flight,
While silly puns bloom in the warm morning light.
With each sniff of humor, joy's gently bred,
Here in the petals where laughter is spread.

Blossoms of Meaning in the Air

Words in the wind like petals they float,
Making sense of nonsense, giggles promote.
Each quirk a delight, a tickle, a tease,
Fragrance of folly, aiming to please.

In the bustle of banter, meanings collide,
With a wink and a twist, thoughts take a ride.
Petals of punchlines dance cheek to cheek,
When laughter erupts, it's pure comedy peak.

Floral debates in the tussle of talk,
Wit's in full bloom as the conversations walk.
So let's swap our stories, come one, come all,
With blossoms of meaning that tickle and sprawl.

Puns sprout from the soil, each line a delight,
As sweet as the nectar, absurdly polite.
In this field of discourse, we're all a bit wild,
Through laughter and petals, the mind is beguiled.

The Fragrance of Insight

In the meadow of minds, ideas take wing,
With fragrances dancing, they laugh and they sing.
Insights are blossoms, bright, bold and ripe,
Tickling your thoughts like a whimsical type.

Chuckles emerge like dew in the morn,
As knowledge unfurls, a curious thorn.
Each quip has the fragrance of something profound,
In this whimsical garden where silliness bounds.

We sniff at the humor, it wafts in the breeze,
With every bright pun, we're brought to our knees.
Blooming ideas with a chuckle or two,
In this fragrant bouquet where laughter breaks through.

So join in the fun, let your chuckles flow free,
In this fragrant oasis, we'll sip on esprit.
Among petals of laughter, insights we'll share,
With each whimsical thought floating sweet in the air.

Nectar-Kissed Narratives

With stories like nectar, sweet on the tongue,
Each tale a petal that's freshly been wrung.
Jests drip with essence, their charm never fades,
In this garden of giggles, where humor pervades.

Floral adventures in the laughter we weave,
With fables of folly, who would not believe?
Each twist is a fragrance, each punchline a cheer,
As we pluck on the blooms of a narrative sphere.

So let's sip on these tales, nectar for minds,
Where hilarity grows, and joy always finds.
Like bees to the flower, we'll buzz through the night,
With stories that shimmer, and make our hearts light.

In this delightful garden where giggles align,
With nectar-kissed narratives, let's sip on the divine.
So come, grab a flower and join in the spin,
With laughter like pollen, let the fun begin!

Veils of Violet Vocabulary

In gardens lush, the words do play,
They tickle tongues in a silly way.
With petals bright, they dance and spin,
While giggles bloom, the fun begins.

Each phrase a flower, sweet and light,
They prance around, a jovial sight.
With puns like bees, they buzz and tease,
Creating laughter, if you please.

In this bouquet of vibrant talks,
The chatter thrives like playful flocks.
With every quip, we laugh and cheer,
Like blossoms bright, we disappear.

So join the fun, don't be so shy,
With witty blooms, we reach the sky.
Let's frolic in this garden fine,
Where words and joy forever shine.

Bouquet of Banter

A sprightly bunch of jests and quips,
They spill like petals from our lips.
Banter blooms in sunny glee,
Tickling hearts, just wait and see.

With humor sweet as honeyed bees,
Our laughter spreads like summer breeze.
Each punchline rustles, making waves,
In this bouquet, the humor braves.

We toss around our playful jive,
In every word, we feel alive.
A garden filled with cheeky charm,
Where giggles grow without a qualm.

So gather round, let play commence,
In our floral realm, nothing's dense.
With every laugh, the colors bloom,
In this bouquet, we cast off gloom.

Garden of Graceful Assertions

In this quaint plot where laughter roams,
Each statement blooms, like giddy gnomes.
With witty whispers wrapping around,
They spring up high, from underground.

A tulip's tease, a daisy's grin,
The arguments dance, just let them in.
Each lovely claim, a petal fierce,
With joy, the heart they surely pierce.

Contention sprigs in playful hues,
As bubbling banter spills our views.
In breezy fields, we toss our words,
Soaring high, like merry birds.

So skip on through this vibrant space,
Where laughter blooms at a quick pace.
Each scattered jest, like seeds we sow,
In tills of humor, let's all grow.

The Essence of Expression

In fields of phrases, we parade,
Each word a gem, a playful blade.
Expressions waltz, in jest they weave,
An artful blend that we believe.

With chuckles sprouting like wild grass,
We toss around our witty sass.
A snap of joy, a giggle's glow,
This essence spills, the fun will flow.

In every quirk, the spirit glints,
Through vibrant tales that laughter hints.
A perfume of delight, it festers,
With every line, our humor gestures.

So frolic here in jubilee,
With playful words, we all agree.
In this bright space of quick conceit,
We find the essence, bold and sweet.

Scented Sonatas

In the garden, bees do dance,
With flowers lost in a silly trance.
Each bloom hums a tune so sweet,
While the worms tap their tiny feet.

Tulips wear hats, daisies are shy,
Carnations gossip, oh me, oh my!
Pansies paint faces, all quite absurd,
In this symphony of fragrant birds.

A daffodil winks, the sun is bold,
While violets blush, so easily sold.
The lilies are laughing, classic and grand,
In this scented band, oh isn't it planned?

So come, take a seat, let's giggle along,
In this meadow of scents, where nothing feels wrong.
For laughter and flowers can brighten the day,
As we dance through the garden, let worries decay.

The Poetry of Petals

Petals chatter in a giggling spree,
While the daisies conspire, 'Who smells best, me?'
The roses roll eyes, all thorny and clever,
In this plot of floral fun, forever and ever.

Sunflowers tilt, gossiping high,
As buttercups whisper what blooms say goodbye.
With each little breeze, fresh tales unfold,
In the world of petals, we've found pure gold.

Violets tease red and yellows get bold,
With each fragrant secret, new stories are told.
A marigold chuckles, "I'm no common guy!"
While tulips just giggle and wave as they sigh.

So gather your scents, join our flowered jest,
In this leafy arena, we all feel blessed.
With laughter like pollen, joy fills the air,
In the poetry of petals, everyone's a player.

Verses in the Wind

Whispers of blossoms tease the trees,
As the breeze carries them, with utter ease.
Laughter spills over from shrub to vine,
In this windy play, everything's fine.

Dandelions dance, like they own the stage,
While the wind turns the pages, the crowd's full of rage.
A thistle shouts, "Hey, where's my invite?"
But the daisies just chuckle, "Don't put up a fight!"

Breezes burst forth with a ticklish touch,
As petals take flight, oh it's just too much!
They tumble and tumble, a colorful spree,
As laughter takes wing, wild and free.

So let's gather our verses, let's sing them aloud,
In this windy wonder, we're all just so proud.
With each fragrant jest, life's sweeter by far,
As we soar through the skies, like petals on par.

Blossom and Banter

In the midst of the blooms, jokes take their flight,
Each petal a punchline, an ode to delight.
Lilies lay claim to the throne with great flair,
While tulips debate who has the best air.

Poppies propose a feast on the grass,
As violets giggle, "Is that really class?"
Sunflowers, proud, with their tall, silly stance,
Whisper sweet nothings, and then break into dance.

Their fragrance is frothy, like laughter it swirls,
As the gardener chuckles, collecting their pearls.
So gather 'round tight for a wild bloom soirée,
Where petals and giggles chase troubles away.

Amidst this rich tapestry spun with delight,
Life's simpler joys steal the deep hues of night.
With blossoms in bloom, and humor in play,
Let's all join the fun, come on, what do you say?

The Scented Symphony of Speech

Words swirl like perfume in the air,
Tickling noses that aren't even there.
With metaphors dancing on the tongue,
And puns that hum like a song unsung.

A chorus of laughter spills all around,
Where silly stories are joyfully found.
Each phrase hops like a rabbit so spry,
While rhymes float and flutter, oh my oh my!

Chocolates and cherries sweeten the chat,
As giggles explode over an old fat cat.
Round and round the banter goes,
Blossoming laughter, see how it grows!

In this fragrant garden where words take flight,
Droll dialogues bloom from morning to night.
So sprinkle some wit and let it take wing,
Here's to the joys that funny words bring!

Daisies and Diction

In a field of daisies and silly rhymes,
Diction dances, having the best of times.
Giggles and gaffes grow with great care,
Words plucked from laughter fill the air.

Broccoli grips the mic with flair,
While tuna fish jokes hang everywhere.
Dauted by diction, yet full of grace,
Our story winks with a cheeky face.

Each pun a petal, each joke a stem,
Clumsy phrases grow like a vibrant gem.
So hold onto your hats, don't trip on a pun,
In the garden of giggles, we all have fun!

When daisies and diction frolic and play,
Butterflies join in, they spin and sway.
With every twist of a humorous tale,
Laughter's a lily that never goes stale!

Incense of Innovation

Incense wafts through the halls of the mind,
Where quirky ideas of all sorts unwind.
Jokes lurking about like little sprites,
Burst forth in laughter on magical nights.

Each concept's a whisper, a funny tease,
Wit mingling freely like a soft summer breeze.
Why did the chicken? Oh, who really knows,
When the punchline's as rich as a field full of pros!

Innovation smells like cookies and pie,
Thoughts twirling like dancers high in the sky.
With every misstep, there's humor released,\nIdeas spaghetti, slurped up with feast!

So spread these scents on the canvas of life,
Jokes launch like rockets, fizzing with strife.
In the parlor of thought, let imagination stir,
As incense of innovation brings giggles that purr!

Fragrant Expressions of the Heart

Love's in the air with a twisty jest,
Fragrant expressions put humor to the test.
Like candy canes giggling on Christmas Eve,
Words wrapped in laughter, oh, how they weave!

A pickle in love with a lemon so bright,
They twirl through the kitchen, pure delight.
Smooches of humor, they bounce on the floor,
While sentiment simmers behind every door.

With hugs spun in laughter like sweet fluffy clouds,
Our hearts beat in rhythm, dancing like crowds.
Each giggle a spark; each chuckle a dart,
Fragrant expressions warm even the coldest heart.

So let's share a wink and a dashing embrace,
Wrap love in a pun; give laughter a place.
In gardens of jest, let our voices impart,
The secrets we cherish with humor-filled art!

Perfumed Prose

In a garden filled with chatter,
The blooms start to debate,
"Who's the fairest of them all?"
"I'd pick the daisy, it's first-rate!"

The tulips shout, "We're tall and bright!"
While violets giggle, what a sight!
"We may be small, but we're quite sweet!"
The daisies blush, retreat in flight.

Pollen flies with every word,
Their laughter drifts on breezy air,
"Let's hold a pageant, make it heard!"
With blooms, all joy and no despair!

What's this then? A garden fest!
Each flower shows off its new hairdo,
Dressed in petals, they are the best,
With fragrance blooming, oh so true!

So take a stroll through this wild lie,
Where petals gossip, truth and jest,
With each soft breeze, they flare and fly,
Scented nonsense, who could protest?

The Language of Blossoms

In fields of chatter, flowers chat,
"I'm vibrant, look! I'm where it's at!"
Petals flap like silly wings,
As they share their fanciful flings.

Daisies laugh with honey bees,
"You can't catch us, we're like the breeze!"
Tulips boast of color bright,
While the sun sets for the night.

"We're the best!" a rose declares,
"Without us, who would even care?"
But daisies dance with carefree flair,
"You're stiff, dear friend, we move with air!"

In this floral babble, sights collide,
Each bloom a bard, with pride they bide,
Scented tales that twist and loop,
Making the wind join in the scoop!

Floral Fabrications

The petals tell a tale of woe,
Of gardeners who left them low,
"Fertilizer? Nah, we bloom just fine!"
Their petals curled like tongues in line.

"Once I was red, my hue was grand,"
Cried a tulip with a tiny hand,
"Now I'm pink thanks to a fool,
Who thought my color needed a duel!"

Violets giggle in the sun,
"You think that's bad? I'm top of fun!"
With scents that twirl and skip about,
They smirk, "What's this? A festive shout!"

"Let's make up stories, blow them wide!"
Whisper the blooms with petals dyed,
For every scent a tale will weave,
In this funny garden, who would grieve?

Odyssey of Aromatic Articulation

In the meadow of ridiculous claims,
Every flower plays these games,
"I'm the best!" the lilies stare,
While daisies tease with floppy flair.

The peonies throw a scented bash,
Inviting all to join the clash,
With pots of color, scents collide,
Like pranksters on a wild joyride!

A tulip said, "I'm great at poses!"
While others fussed with petals' roses,
"Let's spin tales, let's share the giggles!"
As bees buzzed in with happy wiggles.

Thus in whispering winds and bashful sways,
The blooms concoct their silly plays,
An odyssey of fragrant fun,
With every bloom, a laugh begun!

Petal Poetics

In the garden, a flower chief,
Spoke with leaves, in disbelief.
"Why do bees wear tiny hats?"
To sip sweet tea and chat with gnats!

Daisies giggled, trying to sing,
While orchids danced on spring's bright wing.
"Pollen parties every night!"
Yells the tulip, quite a sight!

Lilies chuckled, wearing shades,
As the garden cranked up parades.
All prancing, in flamboyant hues,
They sparked a trend, who'd refuse?

So next time you roam the blue,
Remember this flowery crew!
For petals know the secret arts,
Of laughter blooming in our hearts.

Scented Sagas

A sunflower told tales so grand,
Of a squirrel with a magic hand.
He juggled seeds, a sight to behold,
While the tulips laughed, so bold!

Jasmine whispered to a tree,
"Have you heard? The bee's gone spree!"
He buzzed around, caught in a dance,
As daisies watched, in a trance.

Hollyhocks had a betting pool,
On which bloom played the biggest fool.
The violets wore a crown,
For their giggles turned upside down!

So gather round, friends of the green,
For in the blooms, joy is seen!
With whimsy spreading like sweet perfume,
Laughs abound in nature's room.

Floral Fables

Once a daffodil lost its hat,
Searched high and low, oh where's that?
A bee buzzed by with a giggle,
"Try the hydrangea, it'll wiggle!"

Roses debated who wore it best,
While pansies just took a rest.
A comet of petals flew by,
"Fashion's just a fling, oh my!"

A lilac proclaimed with a zany grin,
"Who needs fashion? Just spin!"
And the garden rolled in laughter,
As the sun played its sunny chapter.

In this plot of bright, bold light,
Where flowers giggle with delight,
Remember, every bloom has flair,
In floral tales beyond compare!

Meadow Musings

In a field of chatter and fun,
The daisies declared, "We've just begun!"
"Butterflies are terrible!" they cried,
"Always flapping, never abide!"

A dandelion puffed with pride,
"I'm the king of the breezy ride!"
While clovers hosted a wild dance,
"Join us now, if you dare take a chance!"

The wind carried tales of old,
Of flowers that shimmered gold.
Laughter rang like morning bells,
In meadows where joy dwells.

So prance through petals, take a look,
For nature's laughter is the best book!
In every bloom, find humor sweet,
A playful world that can't be beat!

The Petal-Promise of Expression

In a garden of jest, where words love to swirl,
The petals giggle, and secrets unfurl.
With stamen of wit and pollen so sweet,
Each line is a flower, each pun is a treat.

Witty blossoms in a bouquet of cheer,
They dance in the breeze, without any fear.
Their fragrance is laughter, a playful delight,
In this verbal garden, everything feels right.

It's language acrobatics, a whimsical show,
Where metaphors blossom and similes grow.
The charm of a quip makes the heart skip a beat,
In this petal-promise, we're light on our feet.

So gather your verses, let humor take flight,
In a riot of color, we'll drift through the night.
Each word a petal, and puns on the vine,
In the land of expression, we'll happily dine.

Blooming Truths and Scented Lies

In a field of giggles, where truths wear their masks,
The blooms all conspire to lighten our tasks.
With petals of laughter and stems full of fun,
The fragrance of schtick brings smiles one by one.

A daisy confesses while tickling a rose,
"Truths are delightful, but lies can be prose!"
With each playful flutter, the blossoms all chime,
In this fragrant debate, there's no reason for crime.

The tulips are grinning, the daisies conspire,
Each fragrant remark ignites laughter's fire.
The scent of pure folly wafts high in the air,
In a garden of jest, we're beyond any care.

So bloom wild and free in this patch of delight,
Where honesty's twisted, yet everything's right.
As petals unravel and giggles arise,
We'll sing out our truths and our sweet scented lies.

Harmony in an Eden of Words

In Eden's embrace, words frolic and play,
They paint up the skies in a colorful array.
With rhythms of laughter and verses that rhyme,
Every phrase is a nectar, sweetened by time.

The lilies all chatter, while daisies compete,
In a garden of banter, they find their own beat.
With harmonies floating like petals on air,
Each tone brings a chuckle, a giggle to share.

A sunbeam of wisdom sprouts humor in scores,
As blossoms engage in their verbal outdoors.
With whispers of joy, they sway with the breeze,
Creating a symphony that's certain to please.

So gather your thoughts in this Eden of cheer,
Where laughter's the rhythm and joy's crystal clear.
In harmony's hub, come dance through the light,
In a world made of words, we'll twirl through the night.

Eloquent Blossoms in the Mind's Garden

In the garden of thought, where ideas take root,
Eloquent blossoms all riddle and hoot.
Each petal a ponder, each stem a wise shoot,
Where logic meets laughter in a colorful suit.

The tulips recite, the violets reply,
With playful debates that could reach for the sky.
The herbs share their wisdom, with giggles abound,
Creating a tapestry of joy, safe and sound.

With honeyed expressions that tickle the brain,
They frolic in verses, like sun after rain.
A thistle's shy jest brings a smile from the crowd,
In this garden of chatter, we're laughing out loud.

So nurture your thoughts in this playful domain,
Where eloquent blossoms will dance in the rain.
With humor as fertilizer, watch ideas sprout,
In the mind's lovely garden, there's never a doubt.

Petals Unfurled in Rhetoric

In the garden of chatter, blooms arise,
Words like petals, oh such a surprise!
They dance in the air, with giggles they flirt,
Who knew that debates could come with a skirt?

With laughter they sway on persuasive stems,
Crafting fine tales of whimsical gems.
A point made with flair, a chuckle ensues,
A bloom of ideas, yet still some confusion!

Oh, the fragrance of chatter, what a delight,
Sprinkling humor in the dead of night.
We argue and laugh, oh wild little crew,
Petals of nonsense in every view.

So let's tip our hats to this playful dance,
For serious chats rarely leave room for chance!
With petals a-swaying like jokes thrown with flair,
Let's chirp with the blooms, for we're quite the rare!

Sweet Perfume of Persuasive Tongues

From mouths full of blooms, sweet words take flight,
Enticing the ears with sound and delight.
Each syllable sizzles, a flavorful tease,
Tickling the nose with a delicate breeze.

In gardens of banter, arguments grow,
We wrangle and giggle, like children in snow.
Bright blooms of persuasion, oh what a jest,
In the hustle of chatter, we strive for the best!

"Oh, listen to this!" and "Oh, will you see?"
As petals unravel, we're lost in esprit.
Our tongues play a tune, a humorous song,
While blooming together, where all can belong.

So here's to the fragrance of jests and of glee,
Where tongues bloom like flowers, so wild and so free.
With each reel of laughter, we craft and we twist,
In this fragrant debate, we giggle and twist!

The Bloom of Discourse

In the patch of ideas, a sprout breaks the ground,
With colors of laughter, the discussion is found.
Buds of bright insights pop out every time,
Spritzing sweet whispering, each line is a rhyme.

With chatter like bees, they buzz here and there,
Delicate stakes of humor float in the air.
Oh, what a folly, to think it's so grand,
To philosophize deeply while holding a hand!

The fragrance of jest fills the evening air,
While petals argue topics without any care.
"Your argument's weak!" someone calls with a grin,
Yet laughter erupts, as the fun can begin.

So let's honor this bloom, this dialogue sweet,
For wisdom's a dance, with humor as beat.
In the garden of voices, where we all can play,
The bloom of our discourse keeps boredom at bay!

Floral Dialogues at Dusk

As twilight descends, and petals do sway,
We gather and banter, in a whimsical way.
With giggles and jests in this floral embrace,
Each joke is a flower, in comfortable space.

A sprout of a pun leads us down a path,
Where each vibrant jest brings forth joyful wrath.
The fragrance of wit lingers, soft and bright,
As petals unfurl in the crisp, starry night.

So let's drink in the laughter like nectar divine,
Each retort a petal, so tender, so fine.
In dialogues blooming under moon's gentle light,
We weave tales of humor, a joyous delight.

And as we converse, our hearts sing with glee,
With floral delights, let our banter run free.
For in each gentle jest, in each tickling pun,
Lies the magic of chatting, in laughter we've won!

Fragrant Echoes of Expression

In a garden where laughter blooms,
Petals giggle, dispelling glooms.
Words dance lightly, on the breeze,
Chasing butterflies with such ease.

A daisy whispers a cheeky pun,
While tulips compete for attention, just for fun.
They chatter in colors, a riotous spree,
Making jokes about bees and their busy decree.

The sun grins down, a jovial friend,
As petals exchange jests that never quite end.
With each fragrant laugh, the garden ignites,
A symphony of humor, in luminous lights.

In this realm where petals play,
We find joy in the silliest way.
For in every bloom, a giggle hides,
Whispered between the floral tides.

The Language of Blossoms

In a world of petals, chatter flows,
Where daisies debate in whimsical prose.
"Why did the rose blush?" one asks with glee,
"It saw the violets flirting by the tree!"

Tulips tackle the latest trends,
While lilies laugh at their ostentatious bends.
With leaves that rustle, their secrets shared,
Each blossom knows exactly what's aired.

A sunflower sways, with a wink and a nod,
"Don't take life too seriously, that's just odd!"
Pansies pop in with quirky delight,
Turning the garden into comedy night.

At dusk they gather, under the moon's gaze,
Swapping tales in a lyrical haze.
In the language of blooms, they find their art,
A bouquet of laughter, straight from the heart.

A Chorus of Garden Secrets

Petals murmuring secrets so sly,
Behind leafy curtains, oh my, oh my!
"Did you hear what the marigold said?"
A titter erupts, "I'm here to spread!"

The daffodils grin, their heads held high,
"Gossiping grasses will always pry."
With roots in the soil, they plot and they scheme,
Creating a comedy, a floral dream.

Joking with worms and teasing the snails,
Their laughter echoes through fragrant trails.
"Let's play hide and seek," the violets chime,
"Where's that sneaky bee? He's wasting our time!"

When twilight approaches, they gather in throngs,
Singing sweet ballads, a chorus of songs.
For in every patch where flowers convene,
Laughter reigns true, in this playful scene.

Swaying in the Fragrance of Thought

In the sway of the petals, ideas take flight,
"Why so serious?" echoes through the night.
A lavender giggles, sharp as a knife,
"Let's spice up our musings with a zest for life!"

The cosmos conspire, spinning tales,
While humor entwines down the floral trails.
"Knock knock!" chirps a bloom with delight,
"Who's there?" chortles another, under the light.

The honeysuckles reel in silly, sweet lore,
Joking about bees who odd jobs implore.
With laughter and fragrance, the garden ignites,
Breezes carry giggles on magical nights.

Each thought is an aroma that flits through the air,
Tickling senses, like love's sweet snare.
In this merry meadow, where whimsy is sought,
Flowers teach us the joy that's in thought.

Petals of Perspicacity

In a garden of words, they bloom with flair,
Talking sweet nonsense while light fills the air.
With petals of wisdom, they'd charm any crowd,
Alluringly bright, but so silly, they're loud.

They flaunt clever quips dressed in vibrant tones,
But one whiff of wisdom and off it just moans.
Like bees drawn to nectar of bright, clashing hues,
They buzz 'round their topics, but never choose clues.

Each joke's like a blossom, a burst of delight,
Yet tangled in laughter, they've lost all their might.
In jest, they convince us with flair and finesse,
That folly's the key to a brilliant success!

So gather and giggle, come near, take a whiff,
Of paradox petals that twist and uplift.
In this field of wit where the jesters pursue,
They'll tickle your senses, all wrapped up in dew.

Ephemeral Echoes of Eden

In a realm where the wise sometimes stumble,
Echoes of laughter make even the grumble.
With fleeting delight, they pirouette past,
A dance of absurdity, fun never cast.

In gardens of giggles where wisdom is shy,
One sprout of a pun can make grown men cry.
A just ripe suggestion, an ephemeral jest,
Can tickle the taste buds, who'd argue it's best?

Yet wisdom does hover, a ghost on the air,
But jokes come alive with a whimsical flair.
Each giggle we share like a fruit on a vine,
A drop of good humor, it's truly divine!

So savor the mirth in these echoes so fair,
For laughter's an orchard, and love's in the air.
Let the peals ring out, as we frolic in cheer,
For wisdom and folly: the duo we cheer!

Speech in Saturated Sighs

In a land where the sighs weigh heavier than sound,
Words drip like honey, just gliding around.
They speak with a flair that confuses the sage,
Each syllable frolicking off a bright stage.

With sighs as the backdrop, each statement described,
Their wisdom's as tasty as pie that's just ribbed.
A sprinkle of laughter, a dollop of fun,
When all's said and done, they've yet to be done.

They boast of their brilliance while mixing their brew,
With challenges tossed like confetti in dew.
Yet deep in their jokes lies a glimmer of light,
A wisdom that dances, though laughter takes flight.

Each chuckle a droplet, each guffaw a wave,
In this pool of mirth, everyone's just brave.
So dive in, my friends, let the giggles be sighs,
For wisdom's a spectacle clothed in surprise!

The Essence of Epiphany

In realms of reflection where notions collide,
Epiphanies flutter like leaves in the tide.
With thoughts like confetti, they scatter and spin,
While reason's a dance that just never kicks in.

A burst of realization, too bright for the dark,
Smack! A funny thought makes its infinite mark.
Dress it in jests, let it prance through the day,
For wisdom that's funny is surely the way.

In this essence of clarity, laughter prevails,
As we ride on the backs of whimsical tales.
So muster a chuckle, and share in the lore,
For learning's a giggle we can't help but roar!

So gather, dear friends, hold your sides, let them ache,
The essence of wisdom is not hard to fake.
Let's sip on the nonsense, toast life's silly spree,
Where epiphanies giggle while sipping sweet tea.

The Sweet Perfume of Promise

In a garden where hopes bloom bright,
Promises dance in the morning light.
With petals wrinkled, the truth does poke,
But laughter hangs like a fragrant joke.

Whispers flit from bud to leaf,
Even the thorns share a bit of grief.
While bees buzz in a joyful spree,
They can't decide on a mockery.

The sun winks at the overgrown patch,
As daisies chuckle, 'That's quite a catch!'
They bloom in hues of cheerful plight,
A fragrant fest of sheer delight.

So come, enjoy this silly show,
Where the sweetest scent is a funny glow.
Promises might wilt, but here's the thread:
A chuckle's worth more than words unsaid.

Dialogue of the Daisies

In a field where daisies chat,
One claims, 'I'm the prettiest, imagine that!'
The next one snaps, 'But I'm quite the star!'
A bee nearby overhears from afar.

They gossip sweetly, all in jest,
Each boasting of who blooms the best.
'Look at my petals, fresh and bright!'
'You call that color? It's more of a fright!'

The wind chimes in with a playful breeze,
'Daisies, oh daisies, can you please
Stop arguing over your silly shoes?
You're all delightful, with nothing to lose!'

So they chuckle, their rivalry fades,
In a garden filled with lively parades.
With laughter blooming in every nook,
They swap their stories, and take a look!

The Garden of Gesture

In this garden of laughter, gestures sway,
Where even the weeds seem to want to play.
A sunflower points with its leafy hand,
While tulips nod as if they understand.

Here, the violets gossip, quick and sly,
'Did you hear what the petunias applied?'
An argument springs over pruning care,
While daisies roll their petals in the air.

Beneath the giggles of the laughing stalks,
Even the pumpkins join in with talks.
'Let's plant a joke under that shady tree,'
'But don't vine-wrap around me, or I'll flee!'

In this garden, the gestures never cease,
A symphony of humor that spreads like grease.
So come plant your laughter, it's free for all,
In the garden of gestures, you'll have a ball!

Fragrant Fantasies

In a world where scents can make you grin,
The air is thick with fun and whim.
A whiff of laughter, a dash of cheer,
Floats through the garden, bringing good cheer.

Petals whisper secrets so absurd,
With every breeze, a joyful word.
'What if we danced like the bees so bold?'
'That could get sticky,' one flower told.

A daffodil dreams of fashioning hats,
While a rogue thistle gets into spats.
The clover laughs, plucking at leaves,
'Let's host a party, no one believes!'

Returning from twilight, a scent so sweet,
Fantasies swirl on butterfly feet.
In a fragrant bloom of giggly delight,
Life's just a joke in the warm moonlight.

www.ingramcontent.com/pod-product-compliance
Lightning Source LLC
Chambersburg PA
CBHW071850160426
43209CB00003B/498